THE ANATOMY OF MAN
AND
THE BODY OF CHRIST

Dell Mavia Johnson Walters, BSN, RN

THE ANATOMY OF MAN
AND
THE BODY OF CHRIST

A Look into the Genetic Makeup
Of the Body of Christ

Dell Mavia Johnson Walters, BSN, RN

Published by
Eagles Word Christian Publisher
New York

The Anatomy of Man and The Body of Christ
Copyright © 2020 Dell Mavia Johnson Walters, BSN, RN.
All rights reserved.
ISBN: 978-1-7336135-9-0

No part of this publication may be reproduced, stored in a retrieval system, or transmitted in any form or by any means, for example, electronic, photocopying, and recording without prior written permission of the author. The only exception to this is brief quotations in printed reviews.

Unless otherwise indicated, all Scriptures quotations are taken from the King James Version of the Holy Bible

Printed in the United States of America

Dedication

This book is dedicated to my family who supported me as I wrote this revelation.

To my husband, Linton, who believed in me, and my two children, Le'Omari and Lanae, who helped to type the manuscript. To my parents, Sydney and Elvita, and my extended family, especially Claudia, Medean and Chanique, who stood by me throughout the years. To Elise, who was a tower of strength, and Toni, who typed the original outline.

This book is also dedicated to my church family, my friends and associates who encouraged me, and to the Kingdom builders who work tirelessly to bring the Word of God to countless souls.

Table of Contents

PREFACE i

INTRODUCTION vi

SECTION ONE – THE HUMAN BODY and ITS SPIRITUAL SIGNIFICANCE

1	The Vital Signs 1
2	The Nervous System 4
3	The Cardiovascular System 9
4	The Respiratory System 12
5	The Digestive System 15
6	The Lymphatic System 19
7	The Skeletal System 21
8	The Muscular System 24
9	The Integumentary System 27
10	The Reproductive System 29
11	The Endocrine System 31
12	The Urinary System 33

SECTION TWO – ALIGNMENT OF THE BODY OF CHRIST

13	Genetics 37
	The Nervous System 38
	The Cardiovascular System 38
	The Respiratory System 39
	The Digestive System 39
	The Lymphatic System 40

	The Skeletal System	40
	The Muscular System	41
	The Integumentary System	41
	The Reproductive System	42
	The Endocrine System	42
	The Urinary System	43

SECTION THREE – DISABLING CONDITIONS THAT AFFECT THE BODY

14	Immobility in the Body	45
	Autoimmune Diseases	49
	Emergency Situations	50
15	Spiritual Protection	52
16	Message to the Individual	56

References and Bibliography.................58

Preface

I remembered my enthusiasm when I first met Jesus. I was ready to die and leave this sinful world behind. Little did I know that there was a process, and that there was a mandatory cleansing that was necessary. Like parenting, the journey seemed like trial and error because churches all have various doctrines, traditions and cultures. Over the years, I have seen members who were seeking God for decades, and when their prayers were answered, tradition blinded them from recognizing the answers. Eventually, they became discouraged along the way because the journey, having many restrictions, seemed difficult. New members also became powerless to the attacks of the enemy and gradually lost their joy along the journey.

I questioned God as I watched a member, who had worked all her life for the Kingdom, die after becoming ill with cancer. The Body of Christ watched helplessly, wondering 'where is God' while the member became weaker and weaker. Some looked on, accepting this defeat as normal, believing on Jesus the Savior and thinking they would never experience Him as a healer.

It was common to be afraid of God instead of fearing God. As such, miracles were rare. After this member's death, the church prayed even more because there was a need to experience more of God. The Lord sent a teacher who ministered to both spiritual and physical needs, helping the church to see the light of the Word. It was difficult to accept these teachings, as it meant letting go of tradition, culture and manmade doctrines. Some rebelled because they feared change, and still have not experienced Jesus in all His fullness. I asked God these questions. *"How can I find You and successfully live in Your presence? What is Your plan for my life and for mankind? How can I help those who are lost and suffering to find You?"*

I was attending nursing school when God responded to me. I had expected Him to respond with a great miracle; however, He said *"Pay close attention in your anatomy classes."*

Needless to say, my anatomy teacher had my full attention, as I could not afford to miss what God was about to show me. As I learned anatomy, the Lord God opened my eyes. I saw into the awesome and powerful mind of God when He created man. He made man perfect, flawless and complete. How great and mighty is our God!

I was amazed at God's awesomeness; however, I still did not grasp the connection to my questions. The Lord revealed to me the perfection of man—His masterpiece: made intelligent, creative and resilient. Internally, man thinks, regenerates, reproduces, cleanses himself, and possesses a compensatory mechanism that makes him self-preservative. Externally, man sees, smells, hears, eats and moves about to guide, protect and preserve the body. The Lord then revealed to me this truth: **as it is in the natural body, so it is in the spiritual body.** There is a natural body, and there is a spiritual body (1 Corinthians 15:44b).

Therefore, understanding the original model and applying this knowledge to the spiritual body gives greater awareness of the wisdom of God and His purpose for mankind. The scripture asked, *"what is man, that thou art mindful of him?"* The Lord revealed to me that **man was made with the Mind of Christ, the Heart of God and the Breath of the Holy Spirit and these made him complete**. He will not only be wise, creative and resilient spiritually, but he will also regenerate, cleanse and self-preserve as members of the Body of Christ.

My eyes were opened at each anatomy class to further revelations. The Lord taught me the anatomy of the Body of Christ. He showed me that the external aspects of the body are larger and function voluntarily. You may choose voluntarily your outward activities, such as prison ministry, hospital ministry, etc. On the other hand, the internal aspects function involuntarily and are of a more complex nature. As such, an internal imbalance can result in life threatening conditions.

Within the Body of Christ, Jesus commanded us to love one another, walk in the Spirit, be obedient to the Word and pray without ceasing. These are mandatory to preserve the Body. Therefore, we must have hearts of love, we must renew our minds daily with the Word and we must be cleansed daily by the Holy Spirit. This is a continuous process that is sustained by the Holy Spirit to keep the Body in alignment.

As I learned more, I tried to hide away from the responsibility that came with these revelations. However, I could not deny the magnitude of these discoveries when I realized the remarkable mechanisms God put in place to preserve humanity. Natural body parts are all perfectly placed, and so are the functions of the spiritual body. *We are perfectly joined together in the same mind and in the same judgment (*1 Corinthians 1:10b).

God asked me to write these incredible revelations that He disclosed about the Body of Christ. However, I had a challenge believing that the assignment to write was for me. I believed that God would find a more suitable writer to carry out these instructions; after all, He is God.

I finished university with a degree in nursing and applied for my nursing license. Everything suddenly went wrong. I cried out to God who reminded me of my disobedience. He showed me that He delayed me because I needed to write the vision. I started bargaining, showing Him all my weaknesses. The Lord said I should write the vision, as it is for an appointed time to come. With that knowledge, I documented all that the Lord showed me. The following day, I was successful in getting my nursing license. Thank you, Jesus, to God be the glory.

Seven years had passed since the revelations and the Lord remained silent. I was happy that He had forgotten. However, the Lord revealed to me that the revelation is for an appointed time and it is NOW. Again, because of fear, I asked God to use someone else. I even volunteered my son who was studying anatomy at the university. The Lord showed me that it is my responsibility to release these revelations. He said release means that I should - **R**un with the vision, **E**xecute the vision, **L**et go of fear, **E**agerly go with the vision, **A**ctivate this vision, **S**tep out with this vision, **E**xcitedly go with the vision.

I put my fears aside like Gideon and asked the Lord to empower me and use me to do exploits for the Kingdom, and so the Lord answered me. *And the Lord said unto him. Surely, I will be with thee, and thou shalt smite the Midianites as one man (Judges 6:16).*

I refused to abort this revelation, and because of God's love, I yielded myself. Many will run who read it, it shall speak, and it shall not lie. It is for an appointed time—which is now. *Eyes that see this vision will be opened, dumb will speak and shall not lie, the cripple who read it shall run and though it tarries wait, it shall come to pass says the Lord, many hearts will be delivered, and minds set free by this revelation.*

As you read these chapters, ask God for wisdom, knowledge and understanding to apply this knowledge of the natural man to grow the spiritual man into His image.

Introduction

And God said, "Let us make man in our image after our likeness." So God created man in His own image, in the image of God created He him, male and female created He them (Genesis 1:26 & 27). And the Lord God formed man of the dust of the ground and breathe into his nostrils the breath of life and man become a living soul (Genesis 2:7).

Man is the greatest of all of God's creation. He called heaven and said, "let us make man in our own image." There was agreement, love and unity in heaven as they created the masterpiece called MAN.

Man was given dominion over the earth but misused this authority and fell from grace. God, as an act of mercy, sent His only Begotten Son Jesus Christ to redeem Adam's fallen race. Mary's labor of love was sent to reconcile humanity back to God.

Thereafter, God appointed prophets, evangelists, teachers, apostles and pastors to reach the lost and to minister to the Body of Christ - *For the perfecting of the saints, for the work of the ministry, for the edifying of the Body of Christ (Ephesians 4:12).*

Man is a biopsychosocial being, made up of eleven (11) systems. Cells, the smallest unit of living organisms, make up tissues that together, make up organs. Organs work together to form systems. Each system has its own unique function that promotes homeostasis or balance in the body.

The Eleven Systems of the Human Body

The eleven systems of the human body are the Nervous System, Cardiovascular System, Respiratory System, Digestive System, Lymphatic System, Skeletal System, Muscular System, Integumentary System, Reproductive System, Endocrine System and Urinary System. They all work together to keep the human body alive.

Their functions are to control activities, nourish and transport nourishment, promote growth and changes, warm, fight against attacks, move and strengthen, produce energy, reproduce, support, protect and regulate activities of the body.

The Lord continued to show me that He placed the head strategically above the body, erected on the neck for flexibility in turning and repenting; while He placed the body under the head to keep it in submission. He further explained that the breath of the natural body is the Holy Ghost who gives life. *Seeing He giveth to all life and breath and all things* (Acts 17:25b).

In addition, the blood that nourishes the body represents the Word of God. *If thou put the brethren in remembrance of these things, thou shalt be a good minister of Jesus Christ, nourished up in the words of faith and of good doctrine (1 Timothy 4:6b).*

Christ is the head of the Church, which is His body. He has empowered pastors to shepherd His flock — members of the Body of Christ. Each member has his own unique function to preserve the life of the Body.

Section 1

The Human Body and Its Spiritual Significance

Chapter 1

The Vital Signs of the Body

The main vital signs of the human body are Temperature, Pulse, Respiration and Blood Pressure. In the same way, there are vital signs in the Body of Christ—signs that must be monitored daily to avert possible imbalances, and to ensure that prompt interventions are implemented, if such occurs.

The *Temperature* of the body is very important, and must be kept within normal range. Temperature is an indication of the health of the body. If the body's temperature is very high, it may indicate an infection- *Because thou art lukewarm, and neither cold nor hot, I will spue thee out of my mouth (Revelation 3:16).* Human beings are warm-blooded, and temperature is controlled by the brain. Our muscles produce heat, our skin maintains that heat, and oxygen helps to warm the body. Similarly, the temperature of the Body of Christ must be warm and welcoming, extending the Holy Spirit's presence and love to Believers.

The body's *Pulse* rate should be monitored for effective circulation of blood throughout the body. Diminished pulse indicates poor circulation especially to the limbs. Relating this to the Body of Christ, we see that the Word of God is the lifeblood for the Body. Diminished pulse or poor circulation occurs more often with laymen who are at the periphery and are more difficult to reach. These areas need to receive prompt intervention to increase their blood supply. Even as blood thinners are used to circulate the blood, the Body of Christ must ensure that the Word of God is broken down to a level of absorption appropriate for each member, to prevent dismemberment. *But yield yourselves unto God, as those that are alive from the dead, and your members as instruments of righteousness unto God (Romans 6:13b).*

Respiration (or breath) in the body also needs to be closely monitored, as proper ventilation of the body is of major importance — *He giveth to all life, and breath and all things (Acts 17:25b).* Any condition that compromises effective breathing requires immediate action in order to prevent complications. Several respiratory illnesses affect the natural body, and the same is true in the spiritual body. When the free flow of the Holy Spirit is obstructed, the Body will suffer from "spiritual asthma" which can lead to death.

Blood Pressure. As blood is circulated to the cells of the body, the pressure should be normal. If the blood pressure is too high it can damage vital organs. Conversely, if it is too low, it results in inadequate perfusion of cells and this can lead to weakness and fainting. It is necessary for the heart to be in good condition, as weak valves can result in poor circulation and congestion in the lungs. The body has a compensatory mechanism that helps to regulate blood pressure. In this case, the kidneys secrete chemicals that increase heart rate. If the blood pressure is high, the kidneys excrete high sodium levels thereby reducing blood pressure.

In the same way, God has set mechanisms in place to regulate the health, growth and development of the Body of Christ — *And God hath set some in the church, first Apostles, secondarily Prophets, thirdly Teachers, after that Miracles, then gifts of healings, helps, governments, diversities of tongues (1 Corinthians 12:28)*. These gifts are part of the compensatory mechanism to restore and keep the spiritual body in alignment.

Chapter 2

The Nervous System

The nervous system consists of the Central Nervous System comprising the Brain, Spinal Cord and the Peripheral Nervous System, which are nerves located over the rest of the body. The brain is the control center of the entire body ensuring and maintaining balanced conditions. The brain is the major part of the head, and coordinates activities by transmitting impulses between itself and the nerves.

The brain is surrounded and protected externally by the bones of the skull. Internally, it receives a large volume of blood and is protected by the Blood Brain Barrier. This barrier allows only selective substances in the blood to pass to the brain to nourish it.

Looking at the Spiritual Body, Jesus is the head of the Body of Christ. Pastors are given the responsibility to lead as Shepherd of the flocks, the church. *And He is the Head of the Body, the Church (Colossians 1:18a).* Therefore, in the Body of Christ, the head (or the pastors), should be specially selected and trained by the Holy Spirit. They should possess exemplary qualities to face the mammoth task assigned. As such, they should be wise, focused, tenacious and knowledgeable in the Word. The role of the Pastor is similar to that of the brain or head that maintains controlled conditions and coordinates the functions of the Body. *Smite the Shepherd, and the sheep shall be scattered (Zechariah 13:7b).*

It is important to note that God intentionally created the eyes, ears, nose, mouth and the ability to think as part of the head. God placed them in this position because of the high level of responsibility they carry. Similarly, pastors and leaders have responsibilities for the visions of the church, and must demonstrate revelation, wisdom and knowledge of the Word of God. They must have the ability to speak as the oracle of God. The eyes are important, because without clear vision the body will stumble in darkness, the eyes being the light of the body. *The wise man's eyes are in his head; but the fool walketh in darkness (Ecclesiastes 2:14a).* The Pastors should be focused, with clear 20/20 spiritual vision, or they will lead the Body into danger — *Where there is no vision the people perish (Proverbs 29:18).*

The ears should be open to hear revelations to direct the Body. *They have ears, but they hear not (Psalm 135:17).* Pastors should have sharp, alert hearing so that God can guide and direct the Body — *I will hear what God the Lord will speak: for He will speak peace unto His people and to His saints (Psalm 85:8).*

The nose should have patent nostrils for smelling and breathing the breath of the Holy Spirit, and clear airways to preserve life. The mouth should always have the ability to eat, taste and speak on behalf of the Body. Additionally, the mouth should eat nutrient-dense meals to nourish the Body — *And not holding the Head, from which all the body by joints and bands having nourishment ministered, and knit together, increaseth with the increase of God (Colossians 2:19).* In light of this, the responsibilities of the head are significant, and therefore, the head needs to be upright, erect and elevated.

The natural head is covered with hair for warmth and beauty, and should therefore be warm, trimmed, groomed and covered for protection. In the same way, the pastors and leaders should have a warm, loving personality that fosters healing relationships in the Body. They should also be trim, active and toned to strengthen their spiritual muscles for endurance. As the hair covers the head, so pastors and leaders should be covered daily with intercessory prayer to protect and strengthen them against attacks.

While the head is glorified and crowned, the body is robed. The Lord promised to robe us with His righteousness. *I will greatly rejoice in the Lord, my soul shall be joyful in my God; for He hath clothed me with the garments of salvation, he hath covered me with the robe of righteousness (Isaiah 61:10)*. The head wears a crown, the highest recognition. *For thou hast made him a little lower than the angels, and hast crowned him with glory and honor (Psalm 8:5)*. Crowning first occurs at birth during the delivery process and secondly when rewards are given in heaven.

The head has the capacity to turn with or without the body. This is due to the flexibility of the neck, which keeps the head upright, erect and balanced. *The righteousness of the upright shall deliver them (Proverbs 11:6)*. This means that turning and repentance is necessary for pastors and leaders daily and is not dependent on the Body. The daily cleansing is more effective when it starts from the head, in the same manner that one washes the face and brushes the teeth first thing in the morning. Generally speaking, we wash from head to toe, and for hygienic reasons, we do not use the same washcloth to wash the face that washes the body. Consequently, if the Head does not repent, the whole

Body is affected. *The whole head is sick, and the whole heart faint. From the sole of the foot even unto the head, there is no soundness in it (Isaiah 1:5b–6a).* **Be careful to note that while the head can see and observe the body it is impossible to see or examine itself.** This limitation deems it necessary for daily self-examination by the Holy Spirit. *Examine me, O Lord, and prove me; try my reins and my heart (Psalm 26:2).*

The function of the head is mainly for the health, development and preservation of the body. *To the weak became I as weak, that I might gain the weak: I am made all things to all men, that I might by all means save some (1Corinthians 9:22).*

The human head houses the brain, which is encircled and protected by the skull. The brain is the greatest and most complex organ, as it houses the mind — the powerhouse — for man was originally created with the mind of Christ. The mind is influential, authoritative and controlling. For this reason, the enemy battles to control the mind because this gives him control of the entire body.

As individuals, we have the same qualities and functions as the collective Body of Christ. An individual can function independently and will fit into the Body of Christ where he or she has a greater calling or purpose. Each person has the mind, heart and breath of God to lead him or her into victory. Each individual can hold the office of his or her calling. However, when working as one unit in the Body of Christ there is strength, security and safety.

Chapter 3

The Cardiovascular System

And the Lord answered me, and said, Write the vision, and make it plain upon tables, that he may run that readeth it. For the vision is yet for an appointed time, but at the end it shall speak, and not lie: though it tarry, wait for it; because it will surely come, it will not tarry. (Habakkuk 2: 2-3).

The cardiovascular system consists of the heart, the blood and the blood vessels. The role of the heart is to pump blood with oxygen, nutrients and other substances to the cells of the body to sustain life. The blood is the river of life of the body as it consists of nutrients in their simplest form and oxygen for absorption. Blood vessels transport these substances to ensure that the cells are adequately nourished and cleansed to remain healthy. In the Body of Christ the blood represents the Word of God which nourishes the Body —*Then Jesus said unto them, "Verily, verily I say unto you, Except ye eat the flesh of the Son of man, and drink His blood, ye have no life in you" (John 6:53)*.

Apostles have great responsibilities, and they represent the vessels that take the Word of God by the power of the Holy Spirit to those even in remote areas, so they can be edified — *Go ye therefore and teach all nations, baptizing them in the name of the Father, and of the Son, and of the Holy Ghost (Matthew 28:19)*. It is important for oxygen and nutrients to be transported to the cells of the entire body because the cells use the food and oxygen molecules to make energy (by a process called oxidation).

This is similar to the Word and the presence of the Holy Spirit in the Body of Christ. Any reduction or imbalance in the delivery of oxygen and nutrients to the cells can result in life-threatening complications. Poor circulation of blood to the limbs can lead to amputation of limbs (or loss of members of the Body). A breach in the blood vessels can lead to poor circulation of blood to the cells. In the Body of Christ, Apostles are the vessels who have been commissioned to take the Word with the power of the Holy Spirit to the highways and byways and win souls for the Kingdom. If there is a compromise in this delivery, the members who are weaker (or in remote areas) will become stunted and possibly cut off from the Body— *Holding forth the word of life; that I may rejoice in the day of Christ, that I have not run in vain, neither laboured in vain (Philippians 2:16).*

On an individual level, it is important that Believers have a deep connection with the Holy Spirit. Quality time must be spent studying the Word of Life. Meditating on the Word day and night in the presence of the Holy Spirit and obeying His instructions promote health and wellness. We are commissioned to go as vessels of God equipped with the word of truth by the power of the Holy Ghost — *That thou mayest observe to do according to all that is written therein: for then thou shalt make thy way prosperous, and then thou shalt have good success (Joshua 1:8b).*

Chapter 4

The Respiratory System

If ye be willing and obedient, ye shall eat the good of the land (Isaiah 1:19.)

The Respiratory system extends from the nose and mouth to the alveoli of the lungs. It allows for the exchange of oxygen and carbon dioxide gases between the body and the atmosphere. The body must produce energy sufficient to sustain life. This is done by a process called oxidation where food molecules are combined with oxygen. Therefore, adequate oxygen supply is continuously needed to sustain life. As such, a patent airway is necessary for delivery of oxygen to the lungs to replenish and nourish body cells. Poor ventilation, airway obstruction, and/or lung diseases all contribute to poor oxygenation of the body.

The Respiratory system represents the Miracle workers who, through the power of Holy Spirit of Life, do exploits for the Kingdom of God. The Holy Spirit gives life to the spiritual body as breath gives life to the natural body. When the breath leaves the natural body, it dies. Likewise, when the Holy Spirit leaves the spiritual body it dies. *And the Lord God formed man of the dust of the ground, and breathed into his nostrils the breath of life; and man became a living soul (Genesis 2:7).*

The Holy Spirit replenishes, cleanses and heals the Body of Christ as oxygen heals and sustains the natural body. Miracles take place in the presence of the Holy Spirit. In His presence, all things are possible. There should be a free flow of air to the lungs. Likewise, there should be freedom of the Holy Spirit to work in the Body of Christ. As breathing is an effortless act, similarly, the Holy Spirit should be welcomed and have freedom to reside and abide in the Body of Christ. *It is the Spirit that quickeneth; the flesh profiteth nothing: the words that I speak unto you, they are spirit, and they are life (John 6:63).*

The Lord God created a perfect heart, brain and other vital organs to preserve and sustain life. However, because of disobedience, sin came into the world bringing sicknesses and diseases with it. Nonetheless, we can still have a perfect heart and mind before God if we obey Him. *And ye shall serve the Lord your God, and He shall bless thy bread, and thy water; and I will take sickness away from the midst of thee (Exodus 23:25).*

How do we live the obedient life? It is by dwelling in the secret place of the Most High where we are surrounded by His presence. We must seek to be more like Jesus daily, which is only possible with the presence of the Holy Spirit. *One thing have I desired of the Lord, That will I seek after; that I may dwell in the house of the Lord all the days of my life, to behold the beauty of the Lord, and to enquire in His temple (Psalm 27:4).*

If ye abide in Me and my words abide in you, ye shall ask what ye will, and it shall be done unto you (John 15:7)

The Holy Spirit must abide, indwell and inhabit you completely.

Abide in me, and I in you. As the branch cannot bear fruit of itself, except it abide in the vine; no more can ye, except ye abide in me (John 15:4).

It is in His presence that we are transformed to be like Jesus. We are the temple of the Holy Spirit. However, we sometimes close the door of our hearts with unbelief and disobedience. Dwelling in the secret place of His presence will give Him the key and access to our hearts. Believing God and being obedient to His instructions bring forth spiritual fruits. *I am the vine, ye are the branches: He that abideth in me, and I in him, the same bringeth forth much fruit: for without me ye can do nothing (John 15:5).*

Chapter 5

The Digestive System

Psalm 86:11 Teach me thy way, O Lord; I will walk in thy truth: unite my heart to fear thy name.

The Digestive System extends from the mouth to the anus. The digestive process includes:

Ingestion: which is the teeth tearing and chewing food into small pieces forming bolus. Then,

Secretion: where saliva consisting of enzymes or chemicals softens and breaks down the food. The mixing process includes churning of food while peristaltic action propels the food along the digestive tract.

The next step is *Digestion*: which is the chemical breakdown of food. This leads to *Absorption*: the passage of digested food or nutrients into the blood. Then finally,

Defecation: the elimination of waste as feces from the gut through the anus. The role of the digestive system is to breakdown and process food to nourish the body and eliminate the waste. Imbalance in this system can lead to poorly digested food, which results in heartburn, acid reflux, peptic ulcer, stomach cancer and/or constipation.

In the Body of Christ, Teachers who impart knowledge of the Word to the members of the Body represent this system. As the natural body is nourished with food, so the Body of Christ is nourished by the Word, Jesus Christ. The

Word is spiritual food. *If thou put the brethren in remembrance of these things, though shalt be a good minister of Jesus Christ, nourished up in the words of faith and of good doctrine, whereunto thou hast attained (1 Timothy 4:6).*

There are processes involved in breaking down food from the mouth to the gut for absorption, and this is known as digestion. This includes the mixing with chemicals in preparation for absorption. In the Body of Christ, Teachers and Leaders should employ methodology to impart the Word to members at the level of the members' absorption. **Undigested food will be eliminated as waste.** Similarly, the Word must be relevant and profitable to the developmental needs and understanding of the members of the Body. *As newborn babes, desire the sincere milk of the word, that ye may grow thereby (1 Peter 2:2).* Therefore, spiritual milk and solid food should be served at different stages of development and at the correct temperature. *I have fed you with milk and not with meat: for hitherto ye were not able to bear it, neither yet now are ye able (1 Corinthians 3:2).* As such, those who teach should be committed, consistent and should rightly divide the Word of Truth to ensure the disciples are correctly fed. The Word of God nourishes the spiritual body, which is exactly what food does to the natural body.

Jesus fed us with His Body. *If any man thirst, let him come unto me, and drink (John 7:37b).* Without food, the natural body is empty and undernourished. In the same way, without Jesus the spiritual body is empty and lost. *For my flesh is meat indeed and my blood is drink indeed (John 6:55).*

What is it that you are feeding on? Did not Ezekiel eat of the roll, which is the book with the Word of God? He did eat and it was in his mouth as *honey for sweetness (Ezekiel 3:2-3)*.

Individually, it is our responsibility to seek knowledge of the Word. We should seek the Holy Spirit who will lead us into the Truth. *If ye seek Him, He will be found (2 Chronicles 15:2)*.

We belong to Jesus who redeemed us with His blood. Fundamentally, everything we are we owe to Him. This means our gifts and revelations are not for us, they are to edify the Body of Christ.

He has appointed some teachers to educate and train disciples through the different stages of their development. As they mature and become independent, they too will answer the great commission, and the cycle continues. *Go ye therefore, and teach all nations, baptizing them in the name of the Father, and of the Son, and of the Holy Ghost (Matthew 28:19)*.

Teaching the Word is mandatory just as eating is compulsory to sustain the body. The body will become malnourished if not adequately fed. The Ethiopian Eunuch, when asked if he understood the word he was reading responded to Phillip, "*How can I, except some man should guide me?*" *(Acts 8:31)*. Teaching is the process of guiding individuals at their level of understanding so that the Word can edify and cleanse the Body.

Chapter 6

The Lymphatic System

Thus saith the Lord unto you, Be not afraid nor dismayed by reason of this great multitude, for the battle is not yours, but God's (2Chronicles 20:15b).

This system consists of lymphatic vessels and fluids that connect lymph nodes. These lymph nodes are felt when the tonsils are swollen. The lymph nodes store lymphocytes, which are white blood cells that protect the body against attack from disease-causing organisms. These lymphocytes produce antibodies that attack cells foreign to the body and they possess memory cells that differentiate the cells of the body from foreign cells. The lymphocytes are divided into T-lymphocytes and Natural Killer Cell, which attack and kill foreign cells invading the body including cancerous cells, plus B-lymphocytes that make antibodies to immune the body against future attack. **If the T-lymphocytes are damaged, the body will destroy itself, as it will not be able to differentiate between itself and the invading foreign cells.**

The Prayer Warriors and the Watchmen on the Wall in the Body of Christ represent this system. They pray and stay in constant dialogue with God working as an army to protect the Body against attack. They identify the enemy quickly and unite in Holy Spirit-led prayer for victory. Consequently, if they are not connected to the Holy Spirit, the Body will be invaded and destroyed. **In addition, if they are not united and are unable to differentiate between the members of the Body and the attackers, then they will destroy themselves.** *I will call upon the Lord, who is worthy to be praised: so shall I be saved from mine enemies (Psalm 18:3).*

The Lord equips those He called and He fights our battles. However, we must remain focused, willing and obedient. Even when the things He reveals to us seem impossible, we can know it is from God because He specializes in the impossible. *Ye shall not need to fight in this battle: set yourselves, stand ye still, and see the salvation of the Lord with you, O Judah and Jerusalem (*2 Chronicles 20:17).

Even while we sleep, the Lord is fighting for us. He created the body with a mechanism that makes it ready to fight any invasion even while asleep. God designed this system for the protection of the body, and for that reason, man cannot control it.

We fight our battles by bringing them to the Lord God of Host. Jesus commands that we watch and pray. He instructs us to pray without ceasing. Men ought always to pray and not to faint.

The Lord placed watchmen on the wall whose roles are to watch for possible attacks and petition God to fight the battles for the Body of Christ.

Chapter 7

The Skeletal System

And He said unto me, My grace is sufficient for thee: for my strength is made perfect in weakness (2 Corinthians 12:9a).

This system consists of a total of 206 bones, whose main responsibility is to protect and support the body. The brain and the spinal cord are protected by the 22 bones in the head and the 26 bones in the vertebral column, respectively. The rib cage, which consists of 24 bones, protects the vital organs such as the heart, lungs and liver. The bones also store calcium and house bone marrow where blood cells are formed. However, disease and inadequate calcium supply can soften these bones and cause them to lose effectiveness.

The bone framework of the body is hard, and made up of many smaller bones joined by ligaments for strength and stability. The body cannot stand upright without the backbone and feet. The backbone is the strength of the body.

In the Body of Christ, this system is represented by the Intercessors whose calling is to intercede on behalf of the Body. Their role is to cry out to God for a word especially in difficult times. They act as mediator between God and the Body of Christ—*I exhort therefore, that, first of all, supplications, prayers, intercessions, and giving of thanks, be made for all men (1 Timothy 2:1)*. In the natural, the skeletal system consists of smaller bones that together bear the weight of the body. In the Body of Christ, the Intercessors represent the backbone of the church. Without them, the church would be weak and powerless. They seek the power of the Holy Spirit and spend time in the presence of God petitioning Him for the Church in prayer and fasting. They are tough and can withstand pressure when they are united.

They are dedicated and committed members who have joined together to protect the Body. They become weak if they are divided or poorly nourished in the Word. In the natural body, the bones are joined together for strength, protection and support. Bones however, become soft and weak if malnourished, resulting in pain and difficulty moving. In the Body of Christ, there should be agreement in prayer, and unity in the church to strengthen and prevent divisions. *Endeavouring to keep the unity of the Spirit in the bond of peace (Ephesians 4:3)*. Division has implications and affect the walk with God — *Wilt not thou deliver my feet from falling, that I may walk before God in the light of the living (Psalm 56:13b)*.

Each member of the Body of Christ is valuable. God has built in us the ability to serve each other in unique ways. We are called to protect and support each other and to promote strength in the Body.

God has equipped those He called. His grace is indeed sufficient to keep us and yes, He is enough. We are uniquely wired for our calling, so stay focused on your mission. Aaron could not complete Moses' task. No one will complete your assignment as you do. In due time you will see the manifestation if you faint not—*Being confident of this very thing, that he which hath begun a good work in you will perform it until the day of Jesus Christ (Philippians 1: 6).*

The Lord my God is enough. This revelation freed me to walk in the confidence of knowing He is always with me. He gave me joy for the journey and peace for the path. Weaknesses often lead us away from God's presence but His grace directs us back to His embrace.

The joy of the Lord is your strength.

Chapter 8

The Muscular System

As ye have therefore received Christ Jesus the Lord, so walk ye in Him (Colossians 2:6).

Man was created to move—to participate in activities that maintain the body. There are involuntary and voluntary movements. Voluntary movements allow man to make choices and decisions. Involuntary activities, such as breathing and impulses sent by the nerves to the brain, should be uninterrupted. If these internal processes are interrupted, it can become life threatening.

The muscular system is responsible for movements inside the body as well as movement outside the body. Muscles assist in stabilizing the body and providing heat. Therefore, we must keep our muscles active to maintain strength and agility. In view of that, lack of activity can lead to atrophy or shrinking of the muscles. The level of activity that the natural body can tolerate depends on muscular power. Muscular power is achieved by a routine of strict exercise. Athletes follow a disciplined program to ensure readiness for the race. Similarly, stamina and endurance are also necessary in the Body of Christ — *Know ye not that they which run in a race run all, but one receiveth the prize? So run, that ye may obtain (1 Corinthians 9:24).*

In the Body of Christ, Missionaries who work tirelessly to reach the lost, sometimes at the cost of their lives, represent the muscular system. As stated before, muscles are needed for movement and strength in the body. Lack of physical activity will result in loss of muscle mass from shrinking. *Finally my brethren, be strong in the Lord and in the power of His might (Ephesians 6:10).* Activity is one of the most important functions of the body. God made man to be independent, carrying out activities of daily living. Mobility, then, is absolutely necessary except during periods of rest. On the other hand, there are certain internal activities that should not be interrupted even while resting, because they can be life threatening.

In the Garden of Eden God gave certain responsibilities to man. He was to care for the Garden. Accordingly, man has a duty to care for himself and his surroundings. If the body remains in a state of immobility, there can be complications that can lead to sicknesses and life-threatening conditions. Similarly, the mechanism to support and strengthen the Body of Christ should be continuous for growth and development of the Body. Just as immobility and inactivity gradually cause harm to the body, unused gifts and talents are eventually lost in the Body of Christ.

There should be growth and development in the Body of Christ. We need to employ the power of the Holy Spirit to establish activities that grow the church, correct imbalances and prevent attacks. If healing in the Body is prolonged, the damage can be extensive and detrimental to the church.

Chapter 9

The Integumentary System

Say ye to the righteous, that it shall be well with him: for they shall eat the fruit of their doings (Isaiah 3:10).

The skin warms and protects the outer body, and is a barrier against invasion. God created three layers of skin to protect the body against invasions and attacks. The body's warmth makes it welcoming, and promotes a state of wellness. The temperature of the body should be warm and the integrity of the skin intact to reduce risk of infection.

The Integumentary System consists of the skin, hair, oil/sweat glands, nails and sensory receptors. The skin, which is the largest organ of the body, helps to maintain body temperature. It is the first line of defense against microbial agents; consequently, it is always exposed to damage from potential trauma. Changes in skin color indicates an imbalance inside the body. As an example, a bluish skin indicates poor oxygen supply to the tissues of the body. In addition, a break in the skin's integrity causes exposure to invading organisms.

Prayer Groups in the Body of Christ represent this system. Prayer Groups strengthen the Body against attacks. They help to maintain the temperature or warmth of the Body and are the most exposed to attacks. As such, the Holy Spirit's anointing should inspire and lead Prayer Groups for effectiveness. Weakness in this system results in invasion of the Body — *For though we walk in the flesh, we do not war after the flesh (2 Corinthians 10:3).*

God's words must come to pass. The Lord watches over His word to perform it and *faithful is He who promised.*

Peter a righteous man, fished all night and caught nothing. Jesus came and instructed him to cast out his nets into the deep. Peter obeyed because he knew who had spoken, as he said 'nevertheless, at thy word I will obey'. Peter caught an abundance of fish - it was well.

Chapter 10

The Reproductive System

But we have this treasure in earthen vessels, that the excellency of the power may be of God, and not of us (2 Corinthians 4:7).

The Reproductive System consists of the male and female reproductive organs whose major role is to produce offspring. The female body is responsible for sustaining the growth and nourishment of the offspring. In addition, it provides nutritious food at the right temperature to nurture the offspring until it gains independence. Diseases and poor nutrition may cause deformity and malnutrition of the offspring.

The Reproductive system is represented by the Disciples in the Kingdom. There should be ongoing training in the Body to produce disciples who are adequately fed, nurtured and growing in God's grace. The Body of Christ should nourish disciples until they gain independence - *As newborn babes, desire the sincere milk of the word, that he may grow thereby (1 Peter 2:2).* Disciples should be fed nutrient-dense meals so that they will be nourished up in the Word of God — *But speaking the truth in love, may grow up into him in all things, which is the head, even Christ (Ephesians 4:15).*

We were created from the dust of the earth, molded into God's image, a masterpiece that the Potter skillfully crafted and wonderfully shaped into perfection — *I will shew forth all thy marvellous works (Psalm 9:1b).*

We are treasures because we carry the breath of life, the Holy Spirit. The Holy Spirit causes us to become living souls. Man becomes mature and reproduces, bringing forth new life. Likewise, in the Body of Christ, there should be reproduction of disciples—this is the mandate of the Great Commission.

Jesus called twelve disciples and taught them as an example for us. However, during His lifetime He made many disciples. Our lives should be shining examples reflecting the light of Jesus Christ so that the lost may find their way to God — *Let your light so shine before men, that they may see your good works, and glorify your Father which is in heaven (Matthew 5:16).*

Chapter 11

The Endocrine System

And be not conformed to this world: but be ye transformed by the renewing of your mind, that ye may prove what is that good, and acceptable, and perfect, will of God (Romans 12:2).

This system consists of glands that secrete hormones or chemicals for metabolic activities. The adrenal gland is one such gland that secretes adrenalin, which increases heart rate and prepares the body for "Fight or Flight" response. Hormones also assist in directing development of the body's functions and are responsible for the changes between male and female at puberty. Breach in this system can result in disorders such as hyperthyroidism, hypothyroidism and hormonal imbalance in male and female.

The hormones secreted by the body for metabolic activities are responsible for changes in the body. Hormones represent Prophets as they have a specialized function in the Body of Christ — *For ye may all prophesy one by one, that all may learn, and all may be comforted (1 Corinthians 14:31).* They play major roles as they receive revelations from God to direct the Body of Christ. In the natural body, a compromise or hormonal imbalance can result in developmental problems and abnormalities. Examples include dwarfism (abnormally short), or gigantism (abnormally tall). There are other abnormalities that are also life threatening. Therefore, in the Body of Christ, prophets or messengers assist in directing the Body to prevent schism or division. *Now I beseech you, brethren, by the name of our Lord Jesus Christ, that ye all speak the same thing, and that there be no divisions among you; but that ye be perfectly joined together in the same mind and in the same judgment (1 Corinthians 1:10).*

Transformation

We were created in God's image, but sin caused the fall of man. Jesus our Savior redeemed us with His blood. As a result, we are transformed daily into His likeness. Moreover, we are called to reach humanity with the Word, which will transform them into the image of Jesus. God deposited visions and dreams in us to help us win the lost and change the world for Jesus.

Chapter 12

The Urinary System

I can do all things through Christ which strengtheneth me (Philippians 4:13).

This system consists of the kidneys, ureters, urinary bladder and urethra. The main function of the kidneys is to excrete waste, excess water, drugs and toxins from the blood. The kidneys also regulate blood pressure by excreting excess sodium and by secreting chemicals that increase heart rate and blood pressure. Imbalance in this system can result in toxicity of the body.

The Evangelists represent this system in the Body of Christ. In the natural, the kidneys cleanse and regulate the body by excreting water and toxins. It also uses its compensatory mechanism to adjust blood pressure and heart rate. If there is a compromise, the body can become toxic — *And purify unto himself a peculiar people, zealous of good works (Titus 2:14b).*

In the Body of Christ Evangelists are called by the Holy Spirit to reach out with the Word where there is a growing need for change. They regulate that change by cooperating with the Holy Spirit, reaching out with the Word to strengthen the Body.

Joy for the Journey

The Body of Christ is stronger as it works together to win battles. All heads, hearts and hands work together to accomplish the tasks assigned. Changes start from within — the mind initiates the change. As such, it is important that the pastors or leaders walk upright and are flexible and not stiff-necked. The head can repent or turn even without the body.

The aim of anatomy is to understand the make-up of the body so that we can keep balance and alignment. The body has the ability to be healthy and to transition well through developmental stages, as it was created to regulate any excess or imbalance by excreting waste and toxins.

Bring your body and the Body of Christ back into alignment. Let each body system work for you spiritually to help you find your purpose in the ministry.

Each individual has all of the systems that the Body of Christ possesses. However, we are more effective when we stand together *(iron sharpeneth iron)*. Each one of us has all of the capabilities in us because we are children of God created with His DNA. We lack nothing—only faith to walk the journey. Let us learn how to walk in victory by carefully observing the natural body to empower the spiritual body.

Therefore, eat the word, breathe the Holy Spirit, keep your eyes open, ask God for vision lest you perish. Listen to God; seek knowledge and revelations for wisdom. Be obedient so you will grow and mature spiritually. Be careful what you feed your mind. Protect your mind. Keep your heart with all diligence.

Section 2

Alignment of the Body of Christ

Chapter 13

Alignment of the Body of Christ

Genectics

The Body of Christ is comprised of diverse members, each inheriting the same genetic properties from God. The Holy Spirit's charge is to ensure that the Body acts as one unit — *So we, being many, are one Body in Christ, and every one members one of another (Romans 12:5).*

Man was created with the mind of Christ — *But we have the mind of Christ (1 Corinthians 2:16b).* He was created with the heart of God — full of love and compassion - *And God saw everything that He had made, and, behold, it was very good (Genesis 1:31a).* Man, also has the breath of the Holy Spirit existing in him — *The Spirit of God hath made me, and the breath of the Almighty hath given me life (Job 33:4).*

Therefore, man is the greatest of all creation; he is a treasure in an earthen vessel, who possesses the DNA of God the Father.

Jesus came to earth to redeem humanity thereby renewing the mind of Christ, reconciling the heart of God and restoring the power of the Holy Spirit in man. In fact, the body of man is the temple of the Holy Ghost.

The Nervous System

In the Central Nervous System, the Brain represents the Pastors or Shepherds who control and coordinate activities in the Body of Christ to maintain life. The oxygen represents the Holy Spirit who is the breath of life, while the blood supply represents the Word, which nourishes the Body. Therefore, if there is inadequate supply of blood and oxygen to the brain a stroke will result which can cause confusion, immobility and result in death — *Smite the shepherd, and the sheep shall be scattered (Zechariah 13:7b).*

The Cardiovascular System

In the Cardiovascular System, the heart represents the Apostles. They are the pumps that transport blood and oxygen to the cells as God sends His Word (Jesus) and His Holy Spirit to the Church. The blood vessels represent Apostles who impart the Word to the Body to nourish it. As blood must be circulated throughout the body, similarly the Word must be taught and passed on to members so that the Holy Spirit can purify and cleanse the Body — *Having therefore these promises, dearly beloved, let us cleanse ourselves from all filthiness of the flesh and spirit (2 Corinthians 7:1).*

Blood supply to tissues can be obstructed by a clot or thrombus. This is harmful, as it results in an inadequate supply of oxygen and nutrients to tissues. This can be fatal resulting in a stroke in the brain, a heart attack or pulmonary embolism in the lung. In addition, compromised blood vessels can result in poor circulation of blood to the limbs causing possible amputation or dismemberment. As such, measures must be in place to ensure dispersal of the Word especially to those who are difficult to reach — *From whom the whole body, joined and held together by every supporting ligament, grows and builds itself up in love, as each part does its work (Ephesians 4:16).*

The Respiratory System

The Respiratory System represents the Miracle Workers, and oxygen represents the Holy Spirit who replenishes and sustains life. The cells of the body get energy by the process of oxidation as food molecules combine with oxygen to form energy. As a result, a patent airway should be maintained which allows for the free work of the Holy Spirit. Congestion in the airways can block oxygenation and the work of the Holy Spirit. Oxygenation takes place in the lungs, which represents the church, where the Body is purified and cleansed by the Holy Spirit. It is the Holy Spirit who gives life and His absence will result in death of the Body — *It is the Spirit that quickeneth; the flesh profiteth nothing: the words that I speak unto you, they are spirit, and they are life (John 6:63)*.

The Digestive System

The Digestive System represents Teachers and the process of feeding and nourishing the Body. Food must be broken down for absorption in the body. Likewise, the Word must be taught at the level of growth and maturity of the Believer. Therefore, spiritual milk and solid food must be served at the correct stage of development and at the right temperature — *I have fed you with milk, and not with meat (1 Corinthians 3:2a)*. The waste or the refuse is excreted, as it is of no use to the body. If excretion is prolonged, it will result in constipation. Likewise, as Believers, we must reject the sinful nature and continually avoid it, or it becomes harder and more painful to be free of it. Malnutrition and weakness will result if members are not properly fed.

The Lymphatic System

The Lymphatic System represents the Prayer Warriors and Watchmen on the wall working for the Kingdom. They pray and stay in constant dialogue with God, working as an army to protect the Body from attack. They identify the enemy quickly and unite in spirit-led prayer in victory. They are warriors who are trained to destroy invading attackers and put measures in place to strengthen the Body against future attacks. Consequently, if they are inactive the Body will destroy itself and be exposed to extensive attack from the enemy — *I will call upon the Lord, who is worthy to be praised: so shall I be saved from mine enemies (Psalm 18:3).*

The Skeletal System

The Skeletal System represents Intercessors who work with the Holy Spirit as the Backbone of the Body. Like warriors, they unite with one goal to protect and support the Body. They combine and surround the head to protect and cover it. They stand united to help keep the Body upright and support the loin and hip. They join with muscles to form strong hands and feet to help move the Body. The strength and power of the Body depends on how committed and tenacious this Team is, as diseases (or sin) can soften these bones (members) and cause them to be ineffective—*Nevertheless the foundation of God standeth sure, having this seal, the Lord knoweth them that are his (2 Timothy 2:19).*

The Muscular System

The Muscular System represents Missionaries who strengthen and empower the Body, promoting stability and mobility. When members are taught and are kept active, they maintain strength and agility. The muscles must exercise and remain toned to prevent weakness or atrophy. The members are stronger when they are kept in motion in the Word — *Study to shew thyself approved unto God, a workman that needeth not to be ashamed, rightly dividing the word of truth (2 Timothy 2:15).*

The Integumentary System

The Integumentary System represents the Prayer Groups that strengthen the Body against attacks, as they are the first line of defense. A breach in its integrity can result in invasion by attackers. Prayer Groups should not be cold or cool and clammy, they should be warm throughout. As such, the Holy Spirit must lead and inspire for strength — *The effectual fervent prayer of a righteous man availeth much (James 5:16b).* Weakness in this system will result in invasion of the Body — *For though we walk in the flesh, we do not war after the flesh (2 Corinthians 10:3).*

The Reproductive System

The Reproductive system represents the Disciples in the Kingdom. There should be ongoing training in the Body to produce disciples who are sufficiently fed, nurtured and growing in God's grace. The Body of Christ should nourish disciples until they gain independence—*As newborn babes, desire the sincere milk of the word, that ye may grow thereby (1 Peter 2:2).* Disciples should be fed nutrient-dense meals with love so that they will be nourished up in the Word of God—*But speaking the truth in love, may grow up into him in all things, which is the head, even Christ (Ephesians 4:15).*

The Endocrine System

The Endocrine System is represented by Prophets who take messages from God to the Body to promote changes, growth and development. They help to regulate the function of the Body and keep the Body in alignment. They are agents of change as they help to sharpen the Body to fight, and respond adequately to overcome attacks. There must be spiritual connection with God for direction or the entire Body will become misguided — *For it is God which worketh in you both to will and to do of his good pleasure (Philippians 2:13).* A compromise in this system will result in abnormal development of the Body of Christ.

The Urinary System

The Evangelist, who helps to regulate the delivery of nutrition or the Word for the cleansing of the Body, represents the Urinary System. The Kidneys, which is a part of this system, excrete wastes, and compensate by using its regulatory system to adjust blood pressure and heart rate. The Evangelists influence change and assist if there is a need for adequate delivery of the Word in the Body within and without. They are wise, as they know exactly the time of need and when it is necessary to act. A compromise will result in toxicity of the Body — *And purify unto himself a peculiar people, zealous of good works (Titus 2:14b).*

Section 3

Disabling Conditions That Affect the Body

Chapter 14

Immobility in the Body

Immobility in the Respiratory System

Immobility or inactivity breaks down the natural body as it does the Body of Christ.

As stated before, God created the natural body to be active except for periods of rest. Likewise, the Body of Christ needs to be active and growing or it becomes stagnant and complicates the natural functions of the Body. During immobility, the mucous production of the natural body is increased and this causes pooling of these secretions in the airways, which can result in aspiration. In addition, pooling of these secretions give rise to bacterial growth and infections such as pneumonia in the lungs. This complication in the natural is similar in the spiritual.

When the Body is inactive, the work of the Holy Spirit is compromised, resulting in Spiritual Pneumonia. Consequently, without prompt intervention, this can be destructive to the Body.

Immobility in the Circulatory System

Inactivity in the natural body causes pooling of blood in the vessels resulting in poor circulation.

The natural mechanism of the body that promotes good venous return becomes impaired resulting in increased work for the heart due to viscosity or thickening of the blood. This has the potential to cause clotting or Deep Vein Thrombosis which can lead to Pulmonary Embolism or clot migrating to the lungs, and this is life threatening. Poor circulation prevents delivery of blood to the tissues, while in the spiritual it prevents the delivery of the Word to members to keep them alive in Christ.

The nutrition of the Body is important to its recovery. **The body must be hydrated and fed high protein diet to repair tissues** — *Man shall not live by bread alone, but by every word that proceedeth out of the mouth of God (Matthew 4:4).*

In the Body of Christ, if the Head is poorly trained in the Word it will result in confusion and possibly bring destruction to the Body — *My people hath been lost sheep: their shepherds have caused them to go astray (Jeremiah 50:6).*

Furthermore, the limbs of the Body are at high risk of amputation if there is not adequate intervention for poor circulation — *And whether one member suffer, all the members suffer with it (1 Corinthians 12:26).*

Immobility in the Muscular System

Immobility and inactivity also affects the muscles of the body as the muscles were made to be active and toned. As such, the body becomes weak from muscular atrophy or shrinking of the muscles. In addition, *'contractures'* which is stiffness of joints results in loss of function and the disabling of limbs. Intervention includes passive exercise and physio-therapy which help to increase mobility.

Similarly, the Body of Christ suffers from inactivity when members become weak with inactivity. Loss of function then requires prompt interventions to restore and promote life and strength — *Having then gifts differing according to the grace that is given us, whether prophecy, let us prophesy according to the proportion of faith (Romans 12:6)*. These gifts are used to edify the Body, for growth and development because this moves the Body forward.

Immobility in the Digestive System

The Digestive System is also affected by immobility, as this causes poor digestion and poor elimination of waste, and results in constipation. Inactivity slows down the body's ability to propel food along the digestive tract. As a result, decreased gastric emptying occurs. When food remains in the gut for an extended period of time and retention of waste from the body occurs, this leads to constipation.

In the Body of Christ, activity is necessary, and includes keenly studying the Word and applying it to daily life. Actively applying the Word of God prevents spiritual indigestion and constipation; as the Holy Spirit cleanses the Body — *Wherewithal shall a young man cleanse his way? By taking heed thereto according to thy word (Psalm 119:9)*.

Immobility in the Urinary System

Activity promotes frequent voiding of urine, while inactivity results in urinary stasis. Therefore, if voiding is prolonged it breeds bacterial growth resulting in urinary tract infection. Immobility can cause further complications, as this infection can spread to the kidneys impairing their function. This can be prevented by increased physical activity and increased fluid intake.

Similarly, the spiritual Body must eliminate and be cleansed of its sinful nature, as sin is toxic to the Body of Christ and can easily spread and affect unsuspecting members — *Let us lay aside every weight and the sin which doth so easily beset us (Hebrew 12: 1).* To prevent this, the Body must be drinking from the Fountain of Life and daily seeking God.

Immobility in the Psychosocial

During a phase of immobility, the difficulty of accepting this state leads to depression, which complicates the healing process. Total dependence on others to complete activities of daily living, coupled with financial burdens, usually places individuals in a state of hopelessness and powerlessness — *A merry heart doeth good like a medicine: but a broken spirit drieth the bones (Proverbs 17:22).* Job found hope and strength in God — *And though after my skin worms destroy this body, yet in my flesh shall I see God (Job 19:26).* Paul reminds us of hope in 2 Corinthians 4:8 — *We are troubled on every side, yet not distressed; we are perplexed, but not in despair.* The psychological state is crucial for recovery. The mind is a battleground that can only be overcome by trusting in God —*Thou wilt keep him in perfect peace, whose mind is stayed on thee: because he trusteth in thee (Isaiah 26:3).*

Depression, Hopelessness, Powerlessness affect the mind and can interfere with activity of the Body. As such, the Spiritual Body must be moving forward in the Lord. An immobile state reduces effectiveness. Everyone must renew their mind daily—from the leaders to the cleaners

— *And be not conformed to this world: but be ye transformed by the renewing of your mind, that ye may prove what is that good, and acceptable, and perfect will of God (Romans 12:2).*

AUTOIMMUNE DISEASES IN THE BODY OF CHRIST

The natural body's defense against invading microbes is the Lymphatic System. It produces Lymphocytes that target and destroy foreign cells. Similarly, God has established Watchmen and Intercessors who seek God daily to help guide His Body against and during attacks. This is downright necessary because spiritual imbalance creates autoimmune diseases. **An autoimmune disease occurs when the body recognizes itself as the enemy and destroys itself.** Diseases such as Lupus, Multiple sclerosis, Myasthenia Gravis, Rheumatoid Arthritis and Guillain-Barr Syndrome are all autoimmune diseases where the body sees itself as the enemy. We in the Body of Christ must prevent the Body from destroying its own cells — *There should be no schism in the body; but that the members should have the same care one for another (1 Corinthians 12:25). Let us do good unto all men, especially unto them who are of the household of faith (Galations 6:10).*

EMERGENCY SITUATIONS

When a person is caught in an emergency situation, it is first necessary to protect the airway, breathing and circulation. Airway protection takes priority because inadequate supply of oxygen to the cells of the body will result in injury to vital organs, and death. Therefore, securing airways and maintaining patency prolongs life.

Once the airway is active, the person's breathing must be monitored to ensure there is no abnormality. An inadequate delivery of oxygen to the tissues of the body, especially the brain, can result in a state of confusion and brain injury. Abnormal signs include shortness of breath, labored breathing, and/or an increased use of muscles in an effort to breathe.

The third step to recovery in an emergency is circulation. This is very important for maintaining continuous blood supply to tissues to prevent tissue death. The brain requires more of the blood than any other organ and relies on ample blood perfusion.

If the body does not respond to this three-step intervention, a person might become unconscious and mechanical ventilation and manual protection of the airways is performed. This places the body in a state of physical immobility.

These situations are also true in the spiritual body.

The 'airways' must be open to the flow of the Holy Spirit in the same way oxygen must flow to the body. Clear airways to breathe in and to hear the Spirit's voice is essential to the survival of an individual's spiritual life. Once the airways are clear to breathe and to hear the Spirit's voice, then it is important to breathe in the refreshing anointing of His presence. Daily communication with Him will activate clear thinking, dispel confusion and enable the Believer to make decisions effortlessly.

The next step for the spiritual body is to maintain a continuous flow of the Word of God. *Man shall not live by bread alone, but by every word that proceedeth out of the mouth of God (Matthew 4:4).* When the Word is applied to our lives daily, it results in victorious living. Absence of these voluntary measures causes the spiritual body to face unnecessary hardship and unfavorable conditions.

Chapter 15

Spiritual Protection

The Armor of God

> *Wherefore, take unto you the whole armour of God, that ye may be able to withstand the evil day, and having done all, to stand. Stand therefore, having your loins girt about with truth, and having on the breastplate of righteousness; and your feet shod with the preparation of the gospel of peace; above all take the shield of faith, wherewith ye shall be able to quench all the fiery darts of the wicked. And take the helmet of salvation, and the sword of the Spirit which is the word of God (Ephesians 6:13-17).*

The Body is fitly joined together, armored and protected by God.

The head of the Body, the Pastor, represents Christ, and he is protected by the Helmet of Salvation. The torso houses the vital organs such as the heart, lungs, liver and kidneys and these represent apostles, miracle workers, teachers, evangelists and leaders in the Body of Christ. They are protected by the Breastplate of Righteousness, while the loin is girded with the belt of Truth.

The limbs represent members joined together, who are responsible for supporting and moving the Body. The hands fight with the shield of Faith and the sword of the

Spirit. The feet move with agility, fitted and protected by shoes of the Gospel of Peace.

The head, covered with the Helmet of Salvation, is safe, and sound. The natural head houses the brain, surrounded and protected by the skull bones. The head is separated from the body and stands erect above it. It is lifted upright to see ahead and high above the body. This acts as a defense mechanism to protect and deliver the body from impending danger. When fully armored the body is able to stand in the evil days against all attacks.

The Helmet is the last piece of the armor to be placed on before battle and is the most important as it protects the head, the control center of the body. Therefore, the head of the Body of Christ, and by extension the mind, should be covered and protected from head injuries by reading and meditating on the Word, praying in the Holy Spirit and feeding the mind with the Word — *Wherefore gird up the loins of your mind, be sober (1 Peter 1:13)*. The spiritual helmet is Salvation. It is the power and assurance that safeguards the mind. The head should have clear vision to lead effectively — *But the salvation of the righteous is of the Lord: He is their strength in the time of trouble (Psalm 37:39)*.

The chest wears the Breastplate of Righteousness. Even as a soldier's breastplate covers the heart and other vital organs, a Christian soldier's heart is covered by the righteousness of Christ and should remain upright — *Light is sown for the righteous, and gladness for the upright in heart (Psalm 97:11)*. The heart is very delicate, so a breastplate should be made of protective material and fit well. The breastplate that Christ gives us is His own righteousness. It not only fits our re-born spirit, but also protects it from any demonic onslaught. The breastplate also covers other vital organs including the ribcage. The ribcage protects organs from trauma and harmful interruptions to their functions, because such interruptions are very often fatal. The breastplate also covers the stomach, shoulders and the back. This area provides the upper strength and power of the body and injuries can result in severe distress. We can see from this analogy that the Breastplate of Righteousness is vitally important to the Body of Christ, because it protects our spirit-man against sinful invasion. It ensures that we are in right standing with God — *Blessed are they that keep judgment, and he that doeth righteousness at all times (Psalm 106:3).*

The loin should be girded with the Truth of God. This is done by buckling the belt of truth firmly around the waist or gut. Therefore, truth should be deep inside the gut — *Behold, thou desirest truth in the inward parts: and in the hidden part thou shalt make me to know wisdom (Psalm 51:6).* The belt also fits around the lower backbones thereby protecting and supporting the body with truth. *His truth shall be thy shield and buckler (Psalm 91:4b).*

The hands are equipped to help protect the body as they carry the weapons of defense and protection. They are flexible and come together to embrace. The left hand is armed with the shield of faith, which is strong, durable and can withstand even the darts of fire from the enemy. The hand moves the shield strategically to protect all areas of the body — *and the apostle said unto the Lord, increase our faith (Luke 17:5).*

The right hand is powered with the sword of the Spirit, which is the Word of God. The sword is the defense of the body. It inflicts deadly wounds and sheds blood as it cuts deep into tissues — *And cursed be he that keepeth back his sword from blood (Jeremiah 48:10b)*. The sword of the Spirit is a mighty two-edged weapon that cuts deep so that no enemy can withstand this attack — *For the word of God is quick, and powerful, and sharper than any two-edged sword (Hebrew 4:12)*.

The feet walk with the Gospel of peace, wearing shoes that are ready to withstand and trample the fire of the enemy. The shoes of peace should fit well so that the body can walk and stand firmly in the gospel of peace. *He that walketh uprightly walketh surely: but he that perverteth his ways shall be known (Proverbs 10:9)*. In the natural, the body walks and moves forward. Therefore, **backsliding in the Body of Christ is not acceptable; as a complete turn is necessary if a person is going in the wrong direction.**

Chapter 16

Message to the Individual

You are fearfully and wonderfully made.
Psalm 139:14

Do not devalue who you are, for you are an important member of the Body of Christ.

Give complete control of your minds to God. He will heal deep within its recesses, then renew it and set you free. When the Lord controls our heart, He has access to the center of our being and deposits His love deep within. We are then able to circulate His love throughout the Body of Christ.

As we eat and digest the Word of God, the Holy Spirit breathes the breath of life into our spirit, keeping us alive both spiritually and physically. The Word of God nourishes us so that the body is stronger. When we are built up and strengthened by the Word of God as an individual, we are then able to strengthen the entire Body of Christ when we join forces together. May the freshness of His breath continually revive your spirit.

Behold, how good and how pleasant it is for brethren to dwell together in unity (Psalm 133:1).

May the Lord strengthen you individually as you move forward daily in Him so that you are able to bring a warm spirit to the collective Body. Let us support each other and provide a shoulder for someone to lean on. May He enable us to protect and comfort each other in love so together we form a bond within the Body of Christ.

Each one of us is a Kingdom ambassador with the ability to make a difference. I pray that the Holy Spirit grants you watchful eyes with accurate 20/20 vision both to fulfill your purpose and to make an impact in the lives of others.

Commit to the activities that build and enhance the Kingdom, including overcoming attacks of the enemy, and winning souls.

God does not want manmade trees; He modeled man to become *Trees of Righteousness.*

God does not want manmade lights, He fashioned man to shine His light, to lead others to Him.

God does not want man to make Him a feast; He created man to feast on Him and His words.

**You are His masterpiece
created perfect — in His image.**

References and Bibliography

Beers, M.H. (2003). *The Merck Manual of Medical Information.* New Jersey: Merck & Co., Inc.

Tortura, G.J. & Derrickson, B. (2009). *Principles of Anatomy and Physiology.* New Jersey: John Wiley & Sons, Inc.

ΩΩΩΩΩ

For more information about the author
or to contact her
Visit: https://eaglespublisher.com/about-dell-walters
or email her at:
dell.walters@yahoo.com

www.ingramcontent.com/pod-product-compliance
Lightning Source LLC
Chambersburg PA
CBHW060853050426
42453CB00008B/965